W9-AGH-688

WITHDRAWN

Nature's Wonders

THE GALAPAGOS ISLANDS

SARA LOUISE KRAS

 Marshall Cavendish
Benchmark
New York

Marshall Cavendish Benchmark
99 White Plains Road
Tarrytown, NY 10591-5002
www.marshallcavendish.us

Acknowledgments

I would like to thank Roslyn Cameron at the Charles Darwin Research Station in Galapagos and John Woram, historian of the Galapagos Islands. You have both been invaluable in answering all of my various questions and pointing me to the correct references.

Expert Reader: Roslyn Cameron, Galapagos expert based in Puerto Ayora, Santa Cruz Island, Galapagos Islands

Library of Congress Cataloging-in-Publication Data
Kras, Sara Louise.
The Galapagos Islands / by Sara Louise Kras. — 1st ed.
p. cm. — (Nature's Wonders)
Summary: "Provides comprehensive information on the geography, history, wildlife, peoples,
and environmental issues of the Galapagos Islands"—Provided by publisher.
Includes bibliographical references and index.
ISBN 978-0-7614-2856-5
1. Galapagos Islands—Juvenile literature. I. Title.
F3741.G2K73 2009
9186.6'5—dc22
2007020416

Editor: Christine Florie
Publisher: Michelle Bisson
Art Director: Anahid Hamparian
Series Designer: Kay Petronio

Photo research by Connie Gardner

Cover photo by Joe Kras

The photographs in this book are used by permission and through the courtesy of:
Art Archive: Navy Historical Service Vincennes France, 1-2, 44; *Joe Kras:* 3, 29, 21, 22, 26, 34, 37, 42, 90 (T); *The Image Works:* Topham, 24; Roger Viollet, 49; *Corbis:* James Davis; Eye Ubiquitous, 9; Yann Arthus-Bertrand, 17, 55; Kevin Schafer, 23; Australia Zoo Handout/epa, 31; Bettmann, 53; Galen Rowell, 60, 62-63; Reuters, 81; DILLC, 84-85; *Minden Pictures:* D. Parer and E. Parer- Cook/Auscape, back cover, 12; Michio Hoshino, 4, 33; Pete Oxford, 8; Tui De Roy, 11, 28, 30, 36, 58, 75; Frans Lanting, 20, 38, 68-69, 70, 90 (B); Konrad Wothe, 72; Fred Bavendam, 83; *Luxner News Inc:* 64; *Peter Arnold:* c Bios Castanet/Hervieu, 76; *Getty Images:* Tui de Roy, 14-15; *The Granger Collection:* 47, 50; *Alamy:* Jeff Greenberg, 56; Arco News, 66; Nigel Cattlin, 78.

Maps by Mapping Specialists Limited

Printed in China

1 3 5 6 4 2

CONTENTS

ONE

A Scientist's Paradise

A volcano erupts, shaking the ground. Lava flows down toward the surrounding sea, sizzling as it hits the cold water. Black-skinned lizards swim in the salty water and feed on seaweed with their sharp teeth. On land are enormous tortoises that lumber across the fields of lava rock, feeding on spiky cacti. Blue-footed boobies waddle across black **basalt** rock, looking more like big-footed clowns than birds. These are the Galapagos Islands.

The Galapagos Islands are located in the Pacific Ocean, near the equator. They belong to the South American country Ecuador and are located off its coast. The Galapagos were formed and are still being shaped by volcanic activity. The islands contain unusual landscapes filled with bizarre plants and animals. They became well known after a visit by the famous scientist Charles Darwin, in 1835. He became well known for his theory of evolution, which changed the field of science forever. Today, scientists still flock to these islands to study and understand their many natural treasures.

◄ *Marine iguanas and Sally light-foot crabs sun themselves on the rocky shores of the Galapagos Islands.*

GEOPOLITICAL MAP OF THE GALAPAGOS ISLANDS

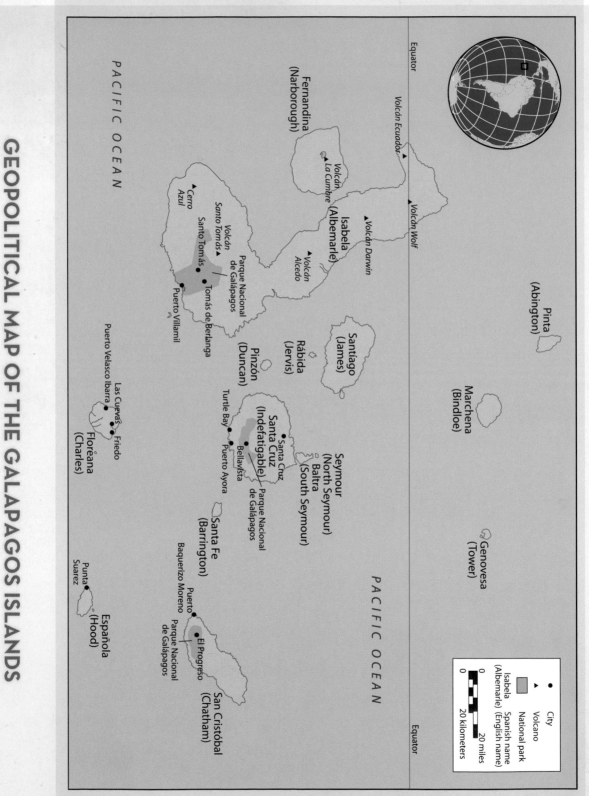

Equator

PACIFIC OCEAN

Volcán Ecuador

Fernandina
(Narborough)

Volcán
La Cumbre

Volcán Darwin

Volcán Wolf

Cerro
Azul

Volcán
Santo Tomás
Santo Tomás

Isabela
(Albemarle)

Volcán
Alcedo

Parque Nacional
de Galápagos

Puerto Villamil

Tomás de Berlanga

Pinta
(Abington)

Marchena
(Bindloe)

Genovesa
(Tower)

Santiago
(James)

Rábida
(Jervis)

Pinzón
(Duncan)

Turtle Bay

Santa Cruz
(Indefatigable)

Bellavista

Puerto Ayora

Seymour
(North Seymour)

Baltra
(South Seymour)

Parque Nacional
de Galápagos

Santa Fe
(Barrington)

Las Cuevas   Friedo
Puerto Velasco Ibarra

Floreana
(Charles)

Punta
Suárez

Española
(Hood)

Puerto
Baquerizo Moreno

Parque Nacional
de Galápagos

El Progreso

San Cristóbal
(Chatham)

PACIFIC OCEAN

Equator

● City
▲ Volcano
National park
Isabela   Spanish name
(Albemarle) (English name)

0   20 miles
0   20 kilometers

Charles Darwin's Theory of Natural Selection

Several scientists prior to Charles Darwin concluded that all plants and animals came from a handful of common ancestors. However, no one could clearly explain how that came to be. Before presenting his theory, Darwin prepared answers for any questions that might arise. He was able to organize his answers through the documented evidence he had gathered. This evidence was retrieved while he was on a scientific expedition on the ship HMS *Beagle* from 1831 to 1836.

In 1858 Darwin's origin of species theory was presented before a group of scientists. His theory presented the concept of **natural selection**, where the stronger and more adaptable members of a species survive, and the weaker die out. This occurs through the survival of the fittest. The traits of the survivors are passed on to their offspring. In time, this causes the animals to change physically. New species with a greater ability to survive—through the development of differently shaped beaks or webbed feet, for example—arise.

Darwin's theory went completely against the common belief of the time. The majority of people believed all plants and animals were made by God as complete and finished products. It was also thought that the shape of all plants and animals never changed throughout time.

The theory of evolution through natural selection created heated arguments between scientists, clergymen, and common citizens. Darwin's ideas survived the test of time. Today, they are still accepted and supported by scientific research and studies.

HUMAN IMPACT ON THE GALAPAGOS ISLANDS

People have come to these islands since they were first discovered in 1535. In the early 1700s the Galapagos were a known hideout for pirates. During the late 1700s whalers and sealers discovered the islands and began killing off giant tortoises in huge numbers to use them as food. They also introduced such domesticated animals as goats and cats. As time passed, people came to the islands from as far away as Europe to escape the two world wars. Many came from mainland Ecuador to make a living. During the late 1900s increasing numbers of tourists began arriving each year.

Today, tens of thousands of people live on and visit the various islands every year. With people come introduced plants and animals. These can harm the unique species of the Galapagos Islands and place their delicate environment in danger. Groups such as the Galapagos National Park Service and the Charles Darwin Foundation have been established to protect, maintain, and restore the Galapagos Islands' unusual **flora** and **fauna**.

Native species to the islands share their home with the thousands of tourists who visit annually.

The unique islands of the Galapagos and their waters are well protected by laws and restrictions.

In 1959, 97 percent of the Galapagos Islands were set aside as a national park. World organizations recognized the importance of the Galapagos Islands, and in 1978 they were recognized as a Natural World Heritage site. In 1984 they were designated a biosphere reserve.

The water surrounding these islands teems with unusual species of fish and mammals. In 1986 the Galapagos Marine Resources Reserve was established to protect this important area. This reserve extended 15 nautical miles (27 kilometers) from the shore and was later extended, in 1998, to 40 nautical miles (74 km). This marine area was named a Natural World Heritage site in 2001.

Today, laws and restrictions have been established to help ensure the future of the plants and animals living in this scientific paradise. There is nowhere else on earth like the Galapagos.

TWO

A Volcanic Land

Millions of years ago, deep under the waters of the Pacific Ocean where the Galapagos Islands are located today, volcanoes erupted. These volcanoes were formed below the earth's surface. One theory on how volcanoes form states that when thick, red, gas-creating **magma** comes close to the earth's surface, the magma causes pressure to build. The magma pushes upward, blasting a hole through the crust. Lava, dust, and ash fly out. Once the ash settles around the hole, a cone is formed. With each new eruption, magma bursts through the cone, rolls down its sides, and turns into hardened lava. Slowly, the sides of the volcanoes grow. They grow higher and higher with each eruption until their peaks appear above the rolling blue waves.

The Galapagos Islands emerged from the Pacific Ocean around five to ten million years ago. The islands are located about 600 miles (970 km) west of Ecuador in South America. These islands have never been part of a larger landmass; they have always been isolated. They are almost completely made of basalt, a volcanic rock. Even today, the Galapagos Islands are considered one of the most active volcanic areas in the world.

◄ A volcanic eruption occurs in a shield volcano on Fernandina Island.

A giant tortoise rests on the rim of Alcedo Volcano on Isabela Island.

A few of the Galapagos Islands were not formed by volcanoes. Instead, they were lifted up from the seafloor by **tectonic plate** movement. The earth's crust is composed of several large, moving plates. These plates are thin and stiff. They float on fluid, hot rock. Heat deep within the earth causes these massive plates to shift. Their shifting and movement cause earthquakes and also form mountains and volcanoes. South Plaza, Baltra, and Seymour islands were formed this way.

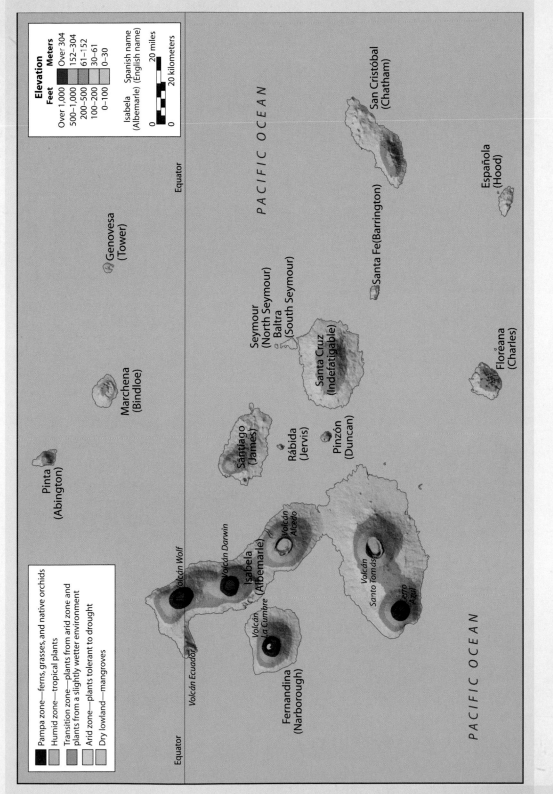

PHYSICAL MAP OF THE GALAPAGOS ISLANDS

Elevation

Feet	Meters
Over 1,000	Over 304
500–1,000	152–304
200–500	61–152
100–200	30–61
0–100	0–30

Isabela   Spanish name
(Albemarle) (English name)

0   20 miles
0   20 kilometers

Pampa zone—ferns, grasses, and native orchids
Humid zone—tropical plants
Transition zone—plants from arid zone and plants from a slightly wetter environment
Arid zone—plants tolerant to drought
Dry lowland—mangroves

PACIFIC OCEAN

Equator

Pinta
(Abington)

Volcán Wolf

Volcán Darwin

Isabela
(Albemarle)

Volcán
Alcedo

Volcán
La Cumbre

Volcán Ecuador

Fernandina
(Narborough)

Volcán
Santo Tomás

Cerro
Azul

Santiago
(James)

Rábida
(Jervis)

Pinzón
(Duncan)

Marchena
(Bindloe)

Genovesa
(Tower)

Seymour
(North Seymour)
Baltra
(South Seymour)

Santa Cruz
(Indefatigable)

Santa Fe(Barrington)

Floreana
(Charles)

San Cristóbal
(Chatham)

Española
(Hood)

PACIFIC OCEAN

The Galapagos Islands are part of the territory of the Republic of Ecuador. They are composed of thirteen major islands, six smaller ones, and many islets. In total, they cover an area of 3,029 square miles (7,845 square kilometers). The largest island is Isabela. It is about 82 miles (130 km) long and is made of six volcanoes. Wolf Volcano is the tallest, at 5,600 feet (1,707 meters).

Marine iguanas look on as lava slips into the Pacific Ocean, creating clouds of steam, on Fernandina Island.

Near the west coast of Isabela is Fernandina Island. It is the youngest volcanic island in the archipelago and is very close to the hotspot where magma breaks through the earth's crust, to the southwest of the islands. The large volcano on this island is very active and erupts every few years.

Galapagos Island Names

Because the Galapagos were visited by British whalers and pirates in the 1600s and 1700s, some of the islands were given English names. In 1832 Ecuador claimed the Galapagos, and in 1892 Spanish names replaced the English names. Even today, the islands can be referred to by both their English and Spanish names.

Island Names

SPANISH	ENGLISH
Isabela	Albemarle
Santa Cruz	Indefatigable
San Cristóbal	Chatham
Fernandina	Narborough
Santíago	James
Floreana	Charles
Española	Hood
Pinzón	Duncan
Baltra	South Seymour
Seymour	North Seymour
Rábida	Jervis
Santa Fé	Barrington

Huge volcanic craters dot the landscape of Santiago Island.

SHIELD VOLCANOES

The majority of volcanoes that form the Galapagos Islands are called shield volcanoes because they have the profile of an overturned shield. When they erupt, lava flows down their sides like honey from a central vent. Layer after layer of lava spreads outward from the center. Lava also seeps from smaller vents on the volcanoes' sides.

In the top center of some of the volcanoes is a **caldera**. This large, round crater is partly filled with magma during an eruption. Sometimes, the jolting of the eruption can cause the caldera to collapse, making it even deeper.

It is not uncommon for the Galapagos Islands to experience volcanic explosions. Some can be quite dramatic. The earth shakes, and smoke and ash pour out of the volcano's caldera.

In October 2005 Sierra Negra, a large shield volcano on Isabela Island, erupted over several days. A tall plume of smoke and ash rose into the sky. Large rivers of lava flowed down its slopes. During the night the sky over the volcano glowed red from the lava flow.

Because of the many volcanoes found on these islands, lava tunnels and pits are common. Some lava tunnels have become tourist attractions. Staircases have been built so visitors can easily view

What's the Difference Between Magma and Lava?

Magma is used to describe molten or melted rock that is deep inside the earth. Lava is melted rock that flows from a volcano, so it is above the earth's surface. Both magma and lava cool to form **igneous** rock. This word comes from the Latin *ignis*, which means fire.

Because magma is below the surface, it takes much longer to cool. This gradual cooling process allows large crystals to form. One type of rock made from magma is granite.

Lava cools much faster because it is exposed to the earth's surface, forming small crystals. Lava creates such rocks as basalt and **obsidian**.

the tunnels. A huge lava tunnel on Santa Cruz has lights that were installed so visitors do not stumble on the uneven surface. In this tunnel, ferns cling to volcanic rock near the entrance. Water drips throughout the tunnel as it filters through the **porous** rock.

WILD AND RUGGED LANDSCAPE

The landscape of the Galapagos Islands is greatly affected by its many volcanoes. Some of the islands are extremely barren, with huge lava fields that look like rivers of frozen rock. A small island, Sombrero Chino, is made entirely of lava flows. Black marine iguanas live on this island.

Black marine iguanas scamper up hardened lava flows on Sombrero Chino.

The landscape on the island of Santiago is an excellent example of the results of the island's volcanic past. Marine iguanas and sea lions wander around basalt tide pools, sea turtles swim in a protected cove carved from lava, and fur seals rest from a night's hunt at sea and perch on a lava ledge.

Santiago's lava flows swirl toward Sullivan Bay.

In another area of Santiago, a lava field spreads out as far as the eye can see. Its swirling surface looks smooth but is as rough as sandpaper. A lone lava cactus grows within the black landscape.

When Charles Darwin first saw these islands, he was awed by the jagged landscape created by lava flows frozen into sheets of ropy waves. He saw valleys filled with large black stones placed as if they had dropped from the sky. He was surprised to find such a wide variety of animals living in such harsh surroundings.

VARIED LANDSCAPES OF THE GALAPAGOS ISLANDS

The terrain of the islands is divided into several regions. Near the shore on most of the islands is a stretch of dry lowland. This type of landscape supports a variety of mangroves, such as black, red, and

The arid zone has a dry, rugged landscape in which cacti and shrubs thrive.

white, in its shallow lagoons. Mangroves live in **brackish** water.

The majority of land on the Galapagos Islands is part of a dry landscape called the arid zone. Plants that are tolerant of drought conditions live there. These plants include several cactus species, shrubs, and smaller trees. Prickly pear, a very common cactus found in the arid zone, is **indigenous** to the islands. The arid zone generally extends to about 250 to 400 feet (80 to 120 m) in elevation. On some of the smaller islands, this type of landscape dominates.

In the higher elevations the humid zone begins at around 650 to 1,600 feet (200 to 500 m). This area is lush and filled with tropical plants because it receives more moisture. Trees grow to heights of 49 feet (15 m). A variety of ferns and grasses flourish in the humid zone.

The humid zone is a moisture-rich environment, much like a rain forest, where many plants grow.

Between the arid and humid zones is an area called the transition zone. This area supports plants from the arid zone and plants that can live in a slightly wetter environment.

Another zone is found on the peaks of some of the highest mountains. This is the treeless upland and is known as the pampa zone. This area is covered with ferns and grass, along with several species of native orchids.

Colorful Sands of the Galapagos

The many beaches found on the Galapagos Islands have different-colored sands. These colors range from red to gold, black, green, and white. The majority of these colors come from the various hued minerals found in eroded lava rock. White sand is not made from volcanic rock; it is made from crushed coral and other white substances, such as calcium carbonate, from crushed seashells.

CLIMATE

The climate of the Galapagos Islands is very unusual given that the islands are located on the equator. The temperature is not extremely hot, as would be expected. Instead, the land is dry, and the temperature is moderate. However, the lowlands temperature has been known to reach 85 degrees Fahrenheit (30° Celsius) and even hotter.

The climate of the Galapagos Islands is unusual because of the low temperature of its surrounding waters. The cause of this is the **Humboldt Current**. This current carries cold water northward from Antarctica. The Humboldt Current flows up the coast of South America to Peru. It then takes a westward turn, toward the Galapagos

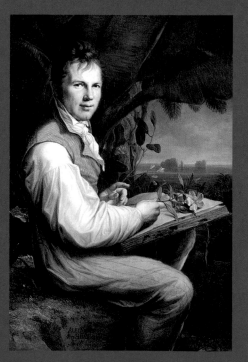

Who Discovered the Humboldt Current?

Alexander von Humboldt (1769–1859) was a German naturalist and explorer. He traveled in South America, Mexico, and Cuba from 1799 to 1804. During his journey, he took careful notes and measurements. These notes included temperatures and detailed descriptions of geologic and biologic findings. He compiled extensive maps of large areas. While in South America, he discovered the cold Peru Current, which was later named after him, the Humboldt Current.

Islands. In some areas around the islands, the water can be as cold as 68° F (20° C).

The Galapagos Islands have two seasons. The dry season lasts from June to December. During this time fog and mist cover the higher elevations. The dry season is also referred to as the garua, or mist season. The average temperature during this time is 71° F (22° C).

The wet and hot season lasts from January to May. During this time the climate is hotter, and the air is more humid. There are also heavy rain showers. Average daily temperature is around 78° F (26° C). January and February are usually the wettest months, but this can vary from year to year. Even though the wet season brings rain, the highlands actually receive most of its moisture from mist during the garua season. Rainfall varies from year to year and between the islands, depending on their altitude. The average yearly rainfall is 9 inches (23 centimeters) per year.

THREE

Bizarre Plants and Animals

The wildlife found on the Galapagos Islands has interested scientists for centuries. Many of the plants and animals living there do not exist anywhere else in the world. On land are the Galapagos giant tortoises and the land iguanas. In the air is a huge variety of land and seabirds. The ocean surrounding the islands has marine iguanas, numerous fish, turtles, sea lions, and whales. The islands are sometimes referred to as a "living laboratory" by scientists.

GIGANTIC TORTOISES

The Galapagos giant tortoise is one of the islands' more well-known residents. The islands were even named after these amazing creatures because they were so numerous. The word *galapago* means "tortoise" in Spanish. Galapagos giant tortoises can weigh up to 660 pounds (300 kilograms) and have been known to live for more than one hundred years!

Even though these huge, lumbering creatures can exist without water for long periods of time, they enjoy sitting in muddy pools.

Giant tortoises wallow in a seasonal pond on Isabela Island.

During mating season many of the females can be found in highland areas. The males live there year-round. One such area is Alcedo Volcano, which is located on Isabela Island. There are several muddy pools there that are perfect for wallowing.

Today, there are about 30,000 tortoises living throughout the islands. This number is incredibly small compared to the size of past populations. It is thought that just a few centuries ago, there were at least 250,000 of these tortoises on the Galapagos Islands. Today, the largest group is found on Isabela.

One of the reasons there are so few tortoises left is that the Galapagos tortoises were captured by the thousands for food. This practice began in the 1600s, when privateers arrived on the Galapagos Islands. The tortoises were gathered up, brought on board ship, and stored alive. They could live for months without food or water, so they were an ideal source of fresh meat for the pirates. In the 1800s whalers and fur seal hunters also began using the huge tortoises as food. Records show that within about forty years, seventy-nine whaling ships that stopped at the Galapagos Islands had taken more than 13,000 tortoises.

Throughout the years scientists have discovered there were fourteen different species of tortoises living on the islands. Today, three of these species are extinct. The various species are distinguished by several factors. One such factor is the type of **carapace**, or upper shell, found on the tortoise. On the Galapagos Islands these giants can have carapaces shaped like domes or saddles. Some carapaces are a combination of the two. The carapace shape depends on the location and food supply available where the tortoises live.

In the 1830s the vice governor of the Galapagos Islands colony, Nicholas Lawson, informed Charles Darwin that the giant tortoises were different on each island. Lawson told Darwin that he had become familiar with the tortoises and their island homes. He could look at a tortoise and know which island was its home. This observation turned out to be true.

Because there is plenty of low-lying food available in the

The saddle-back giant tortoise has a long neck, allowing it to eat high-growing vegetation.

highlands, the huge dome-shelled tortoises living in this environment have short necks and legs. They have no need to reach up to grab food. Their carapace has evolved over time to help them push through the vegetation. The smaller saddle-backed tortoises live on islands that are lowlands. Food can be scarce in this dry area. Their carapace evolved into the saddle-back shape, which has a higher opening for the neck. In addition, these tortoises developed longer necks and legs. All three factors allow the tortoises to lift their heads and bodies to eat higher-growing vegetation.

The Galapagos giant tortoise has no teeth but has a curved mouth that is very strong. These two characteristics help it to eat tough vegetation such as cacti. Its thick and scaly feet help the tortoise move its heavy body over different types of terrain, from its nesting area in the lowlands to the moist vegetation in the highlands. As it slowly moves from place to place, its thick shell makes a dull thumping sound as it strikes against lava rocks.

If a tortoise becomes startled, it pulls its head and legs into its shell. While doing this, it makes a loud hissing sound similar to air coming out of a tire.

These tortoises have a **symbiotic** relationship with Darwin's finches and mockingbirds. The tortoise rids itself of pesky bugs by standing up and stretching out its neck. This allows the finches or mockingbirds to peck at the tortoise's skin for a tasty meal.

Two Famous Tortoises

There are two famous tortoises on the Galapagos Islands: Harriet and Lonesome George. Harriet (right) was probably born around 1830. It is thought that she was picked up by the HMS *Beagle*, the ship with Charles Darwin on board. When Harriet was first found, she was about the size of a dinner plate. By 2005 she had grown to about 3 square feet (0.28 m), which is as  big as a small couch! She was very heavy, at 330 pounds (150 kg). Throughout the years she became quite a celebrity. On her 175th birthday, the Australia Zoo had a party for her that included a tortoise-shaped cake. She died in June 2006 of a heart attack. At 176 years old, she was one of the oldest known living creatures in the world.

Lonesome George is another famous tortoise. He was found on Pinta Island in 1972 and is the last known remaining Pinta tortoise. He was taken to the Charles Darwin Research Station in Puerto Ayora, Santa Cruz, with the hope of finding him a mate. He remains at the station today, sharing his corral with two females from Wolf Volcano on Isabela Island. These females are physically very similar to the species found on Pinta Island. So far, Lonesome George has failed to produce offspring with the females. If he dies without offspring, he will be the last of the unique species once found on Pinta Island.

Bizarre Lizards

Iguanas can be found throughout Central and South America. However, the iguanas found on the Galapagos Islands are **endemic** and can only be found there. Perhaps the lizards originally arrived on the Galapagos Islands on floating rafts of vegetation or driftwood from mainland South and Central America. Once they arrived, over time they eventually adapted to the rough terrain by developing unusual methods for survival.

Living in the drier areas of the islands is the land iguana. This yellow iguana weighs up to 29 pounds (13 kg), about as heavy as a large cat. It can reach a length more than 3 feet (1 m). The land iguana's main food source is cacti. It eats the flowers and flesh, spines and all! This iguana can survive its dry habitat because it gets water from the cacti.

On the island of Fernandina, female land iguanas risk their lives to lay their eggs. They climb down the steep cliffs of the volcanoes to where the ground is warm. Once the young hatch, hawks and snakes are waiting to eat them. If the newly-hatched land iguanas survive, they must climb up the steep cliffs and hike miles back to where the adult land iguanas live. The first several years of life are the most difficult. Even so, these iguanas can live to be up to sixty years old.

When Darwin and his companions first arrived on the Galapagos Islands, these lizards were numerous. Because there were so many land iguana burrows, Darwin had a hard time finding a flat spot to set up his tent.

There are two species of land iguana on the Galapagos. Both feed on plants and shrubs and are territorial.

Today that is not the case. On Baltra Island land iguanas completely disappeared after World War II. Scientists believe part of the problem was caused by **feral** cats. These cats had been known to kill young iguanas. Since 1970 land iguanas have been bred in captivity at the Charles Darwin Research Station. Once the land iguanas are large enough to escape cats, they are **repatriated**. By 2004 all feral cats were removed to ensure the future of land iguanas on Baltra. Scientists are excited by the recent natural growth of the land iguana population there.

A common lizard on the Galapagos Islands is the marine iguana. It is the only lizard in the world that feeds in the sea. More than 200,000

During mating season male marine iguanas change color to red and green.

of these lizards can be found on the rocky seashores throughout the various islands. The marine iguana's color and size vary from island to island, but all are considered one species. The smallest marine iguanas can be found in the far north, on Genovesa Island. The largest can be found on Isabela, growing to about 4 feet (1 m). Depending on their location, their coloring ranges from black to dark gray.

These iguanas live on land but eat algae found in the ocean. Their teeth have developed to help them cut through algae. Marine iguanas have also been known to eat droppings from such other animals as sea lions, crabs, and other marine iguanas.

While feeding in the salty seawater, marine iguanas take in a lot of salt. They have glands located above their eyes that remove the salt from the water. The salt is then sneezed out of their salt glands.

During mating season, which lasts from December to January, male marine iguanas turn colors, to red and green. Because of this, locals jokingly call them Christmas iguanas. Females lay eggs near the end of the warm season, around March and April. They dig burrows in the sand and lay up to four eggs. It takes about four mouths for the eggs to hatch.

Lava lizards are also found on the islands. There are seven different species of them. However, it is thought that all species of lava lizards come from one ancestor. It is easy to tell the males and females apart, as their skin texture and body size are not the same. Males are usually much larger and have more textured skin. Depending on the species, both males and females may have a red throat.

Unusual and Rare Birds

The abundant animal life on the Galapagos Islands also includes birds. There are twenty-nine species of land birds, such as the Galapagos hawk, red-billed tropicbird, Galapagos mockingbird, and greater flamingo. There are also nineteen species of seabirds, including the waved albatross, lava gull, and frigate bird. Of these, twenty-two species of land birds and five species of seabirds are endemic—only found on the Galapagos Islands. Some of the most unusual are boobies, flightless cormorants, Galapagos penguins, and Darwin's finches.

There are three species of boobies living on the Galapagos Islands: the blue-footed booby, the red-footed booby, and the Nazca booby. They may appear awkward on land, but in the air and water they are graceful and quick.

A blue-footed booby "dances" during its courtship ritual.

Watching a blue-footed booby catch fish is very exciting. It starts its dive at around 49 feet (15 m) in the air. As it gets closer to the water, it folds its wings, forming a shape like a missile. Once in the water the booby chases fish by using its wings and feet to steer itself. It usually resurfaces several yards away from its dive site with a fish in its mouth.

The mating dance of boobies is quite comical. Both males and females move their blue feet up and down while, at the same time, the females honk and the males whistle.

Cormorants are found throughout the world. However, only one species, the flightless cormorant, can be found on the Galapagos Islands. These cormorants are the only ones that have lost the ability to fly. Flightless cormorants had no natural predators on the Galapagos and eventually lost the use of their wings, as they did not need to fly. Their legs are thicker and much stronger than those of other cormorants. They use their strong legs to move through the water with powerful kicks. Their streamlined bodies are very useful for swimming and diving. These abilities help them catch eel, fish, and octopus. Flightless cormorants can only be found around western Isabela and Fernandina islands.

Galapagos penguins are among the smallest penguins in the world, at 20 inches (50 cm) tall. They are also the only penguins found near the equator. This bird can be found around Fernandina, Isabela, Santiago, Sombrero Chino, and Bartolomé islands. These penguins do not nest in large colonies. They are often found living in cracks and crannies along the rocky shorelines. Because of the Humboldt

No other penguin lives as far north as the Galapagos penguin.

Current, some of the waters surrounding the Galapagos Islands stay cool, which is perfect for penguins. Instead of protecting themselves from the cold, they must protect themselves from the heat. They have been known to stretch out their short wings, shading their feet to protect them from getting sunburned.

A cactus finch sips nectar from a flower on the Galapagos Islands.

DARWIN'S FINCHES

One of the most important observations Charles Darwin made after his visit to the Galapagos Islands was that there was a wide variety of finches living there. He identified thirteen types of finches by their unique beaks. Each finch had developed a different beak shape, depending on its diet. Some finches ate nectar and pollen, while others ate seeds. Other finches landed on iguanas and tortoises to pick insects off their skin. One type of finch used a twig as a tool to dig for grubs buried in tree branches. Another type rolled thick-shelled seabird eggs off cliffs to break them open. This allowed the finch to get at the yolk inside.

The most unusual of these finches is nicknamed the vampire finch. This finch is known to use its pointed beak to peck at the tail of a bird until it begins to bleed. Once the blood drops appear, it sips them up.

Today, it is not uncommon to find finches and other birds on the islands with small identification bands around their legs. These birds are being studied by scientists at the Charles Darwin Research Station. Scientists study such things as behavior, feeding patterns, and the impact on population size of introduced species.

SEA LIFE OF THE GALAPAGOS

The water surrounding the Galapagos Islands is teeming with sea life. Some animals found there are Pacific green turtles, hawksbill turtles, leatherback turtles, olive ridley turtles, Galapagos fur seals, sperm whales, humpback whales, and orcas. Near the reefs and shores are mustard stingrays, huge parrot fish, and whitetip sharks. Spotted moray eels can be found hiding in small sea caves. Scorpion fish camouflage themselves in the rocks. Sea horses swim among sea plants. Starfish, such as the chocolate chip sea star, are brilliantly colored in orange and yellow and dotted with thick black spikes.

Sea turtles are abundant in the Galapagos Islands. They can be seen swimming on the surface or underwater. Several of the islands contain turtle nesting areas. They are easy to spot, as there are huge drag marks in the sand leading up to wide indentations. The holes are the nests, and no one is allowed to approach them.

One of the most common sea animals is the Galapagos sea lion. The Galapagos sea lion is similar to the California sea lion. Sea lions live in groups called harems, which include an aggressive male called a bull, females called cows, and young called pups. The male protects his territory, which is usually a small bay, cove, or beach. Bulls are very protective of their territory. They

There are about 50,000 Galapagos sea lions living among the islands.

patrol their area and bark loudly. They will fight any approaching males that stray into their domain.

Pups usually stay in shallow water. This area is rcfcrred to as the nursery. Young sea lions swim and play among the rocky shores for hours at a time. When hungry, pups bleat to encourage their mothers to return to feed them.

Plants

Unique animals are not the only wild things found on the Galapagos Islands. There are unusual plants as well. On some islands carpet-weed is found on the ground. Land iguanas feed on its flowers and fleshy leaves. In the arid and transitional zones the most dramatic plant is the giant prickly pear cactus. Fourteen varieties of this cactus have evolved throughout the different islands. Depending on the island, the prickly pear might grow right out of the lava rock. The tallest prickly pear is found on Santa Cruz Island. It can grow up to 40 feet (12 m) high.

When this cactus first starts to grow, its trunk is densely covered with long spines that point downward. It is thought the spines protect the young plant from being eaten by land iguanas and tortoises.

Prickly pear cactus is the most common cactus found in the Galapagos.

As the cactus matures, the spines fall off. The pads of the cactus eventually join and harden into a brown bark. This bark forms a trunk around the soft, spongelike center. The pads and fruit of this cactus are a very important part of the land iguanas and giant tortoise's diet.

Another bizarre cactus found in the arid zone is the lava cactus. It is the smallest cactus found on the Galapagos Islands. It can only be found in barren stretches of lava fields. The lava cactus is made of many short, prickly stems. When the stems first develop, they are a greenish yellow color, and they turn black as they age.

A tree to be wary of is the poison apple tree. It has large leaves and small green fruit that smell and look just like apples. Its sap is poisonous and will burn the skin on contact. Visitors are warned not to sit under this tree for shade and not to touch or eat the fruit.

Many introduced plants grow in the humid zone. These plants include the quinine tree, grown to produce the malaria medicine quinine; the common guava, which grows edible fruit; and the Spanish cedar tree. This tree was introduced to provide wood for building. Because of the overabundance of these introduced plants, the endemic *Miconia* shrub—which provides excellent nesting sites for the rare Galapagos petrel—is threatened.

A variety of ferns also grow in the humid zone. The tallest is the Galapagos tree fern. This fern can grow to almost 10 feet (3 m) high, with a trunk 12 inches (30 cm) in diameter. It is topped with thick, 7- to 10-foot- (2- to 3-m-) long fern branches that look like palm fronds.

FOUR

Pirates and Whalers

The first recorded human contact with the Galapagos Islands was made by the bishop of Panama, Fray Tomás de Berlanga. He set sail from Panama to Peru in 1535. On the way the wind died down, so the ship drifted helplessly for several days. Eventually, freshwater ran very low on board. The passengers and animals began to suffer from thirst. The strong Humboldt Current pulled the ship far off its course. It was carried to volcanic islands with strange animals living on them. These islands became known as the Galapagos Islands.

The ship stopped at these forbidding islands so its crew could search for water. However, it took several days for any freshwater to be found. In the meantime, a man and ten horses died of thirst. While searching for water, the crew discovered that prickly pear cactus pads contained drinkable liquid that could be squeezed out.

During Berlanga's visit, he could not help but notice the enormous tortoises. This observation may have been why the name Insulae de los Galopegos, or Islands of the Tortoises, was printed on a world map in 1569.

This watercolor depicts Galapagos giant tortoises as seen by a late-seventeenth-century sea captain.

Ancient Post Office of the Galapagos Islands

On Floreana Island is an ancient post office—a barrel nailed to a pole. It was created in the late 1700s by sailors working on whaling ships. They did not have the means to communicate with loved ones at home. The barrel on Floreana became a good way to solve this problem. Letters were put into the barrel with the hope that other sailors would look through the letters. If there were any letters with addresses close to their destination, they could be hand-delivered. Floreana's postal service was a courtesy between sailors working on different ships.

Tourists carry on this tradition today. Visitors to Floreana still check the old mail barrel for letters addressed to people living close to their homes. If there are any, they are hand-delivered to the recipients.

Some sailors called the islands Las Encantadas, meaning Enchanted Islands, because of the strong currents surrounding the islands and the misty fog that covered them. Sailors were under the impression that the islands moved on their own from place to place.

During the 1500s Spain began accumulating huge amounts of wealth from its growing empire. At this time the Spanish showed little interest in the Galapagos Islands because of their lack of water. Establishing settlements and farms would be extremely difficult in this region. Spain's growing power threatened other European countries, including England. English **privateers** began attacking Spanish ships, especially those headed back to Spain filled with wealth from the New World. Until the early 1700s the Galapagos Islands were the perfect hideout for marauding privateers.

As sailors explored the Pacific Ocean, they became familiar with the Humboldt Current. The cold water of this current was filled with plankton that was consumed in huge quantities by baleen whales.

In the late 1700s to the mid-1800s, American, British, and European whalers roamed the Pacific Ocean. Sometimes they were at sea for months or years at a time. Because of this, obtaining fresh food was a constant problem. Unfortunately, the Galapagos giant tortoises were the perfect solution. Whalers often anchored their ships at the islands and stocked up with hundreds of tortoises, to be eaten later.

The waters off the coast of South America were favorite whaling grounds during the 1700s and 1800s.

Whalers and privateers visited the islands for about two hundred years. During this time the damage done to the wildlife was massive. Whales were slaughtered in huge numbers off the shores. Fur seals were hunted almost to extinction. Huge numbers of tortoises were killed or taken for food. Domesticated animals, such as goats, dogs, and cats, were also introduced.

Galapagos's First Settler

The first person known to have settled on Floreana was an Irishman named Patrick Watkins. He arrived in the early 1800s. There are many stories that speculate how he got to the Galapagos Islands. Some stories claim he was marooned, and others say that he arrived on the islands voluntarily. It is known that while on the island, he raised potatoes and pumpkins, which he sold for cash or exchanged for rum with passing ships. There are also different versions regarding the length of his stay on the island. However, it is known that he was not on Floreana in 1813. He left by sailing away from the Galapagos Islands and arriving on the mainland.

The Galapagos Islands became settled during the 1800s. This is a view of San Cristóbal at that time.

ECUADOR AND THE GALAPAGOS ISLANDS

In 1832 the Galapagos Islands were claimed by Ecuador. Meanwhile, a Frenchman from Louisiana named Jose Villamil went to Ecuador with the hopes of establishing settlements on the Galapagos Islands. He persuaded the Ecuadorian government to grant him a **concession,** in 1833, to settle Floreana.

Villamil brought in convicts from mainland Ecuador to work the land. He also recruited workers in Guayaquil, the main port city on mainland Ecuador, to live on the islands. The new settlers began raising cattle, pigs, and goats, as well as growing fruits and vegetables.

The village was later turned into a **penal colony**. History continued to repeat itself over the next hundred years with attempts at settlements that would then turn into penal colonies.

Efforts were made to capitalize on some of the Galapagos Islands' natural resources. They involve commercial fishing, mining for salt, and retrieving oil from the Galapagos giant tortoises, which could be used for cooking and filling oil lamps.

Charles Darwin's theory of natural selection was based on what he saw on the Galapagos Islands.

CHARLES DARWIN'S FAMOUS VOYAGE

The most famous visitor to the Galapagos Islands was the scientist Charles Darwin. His theory of natural selection was inspired by what he saw and collected during the five weeks he visited the islands. This theory transformed biology and is still accepted today.

Charles Darwin was twenty-two years old when he began planning his trip, in late August 1831. He was set to travel on HMS *Beagle* under the command of Captain Robert FitzRoy. The ship was to be gone for two years on a British scientific expedition. The purpose of the journey was to survey Patagonia, a

MAP OF DARWIN'S EXPEDITION, 1831–1835

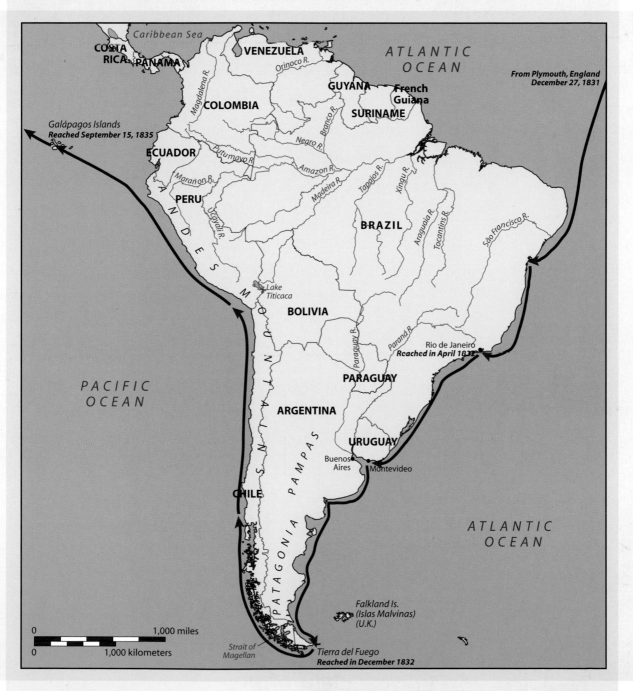

Caribbean Sea

COSTA RICA
PANAMA
VENEZUELA

ATLANTIC OCEAN

From Plymouth, England
December 27, 1831

Orinoco R.

GUYANA
French Guiana
SURINAME

COLOMBIA

Magdalena R.

Galápagos Islands
Reached September 15, 1835

ECUADOR

Branco R.

Negro R.

Putumayo R.

Amazon R.

Marañon R.

PERU

Ucayali R.

Madeira R.

Tapajos R.

Xingu R.

Araguaia R.

Tocantins R.

São Francisco R.

A N D E S

BRAZIL

PACIFIC OCEAN

Lake Titicaca

M O U N T A I N S

BOLIVIA

Paraguay R.

Paraná R.

Rio de Janeiro
Reached in April 1832

PARAGUAY

ARGENTINA

URUGUAY

Buenos Aires
Montevideo

CHILE

P A T A G O N I A   P A M P A S

ATLANTIC OCEAN

0 ————— 1,000 miles
0 ————— 1,000 kilometers

Falkland Is.
(Islas Malvinas)
(U.K.)

Strait of Magellan

Tierra del Fuego
Reached in December 1832

barren region of Argentina and Chile, as well as the shores of Chile and Peru. There were also plans to visit several Pacific islands.

Darwin was invited to come as a **naturalist**. During the journey he would collect specimens and study rocks, animals, and plants. He packed many tools to assist him in his scientific discoveries, including microscopes, pickling fluid, various glass vials and containers, and preserving paper. The sea voyage continued far longer than expected. Charles Darwin was gone for five years.

Even though Darwin traveled in very uncomfortable conditions and often got sick, he was fascinated by his scientific discoveries. While in South America Darwin gathered fossils of gigantic extinct species.

The earth shook from volcanic eruptions while Darwin was in Chile. He observed the earth shifting. From this observation, he established that the earth's crust could be pushed up or pulled down several thousand feet.

In September 1835 Charles Darwin arrived on the Galapagos Islands. His first impression was that the islands were a very uninviting place. Black-skinned lizards and bright orange crabs scrambled under his feet as he climbed over sharp lava rock. While visiting the islands, one main complaint from Darwin and his companions was the constant lack of water. He wrote in his diary, "The main evil under which these islands suffer is the scarcity of water."

While visiting the island of Isabela, he was thrilled to discover what looked like a freshwater lake. He quickly made his way to its shore.

Charles Darwin explored the Galapagos Islands, documenting his finds and discoveries.

Once there he scooped up the water and drank it. Immediately, he spat out what turned out to be salty water. This lake, which is at Tagus Cove, was later named Darwin Lake.

The flora and fauna kept Darwin interested and excited. On the islands he observed that there were two species of iguana. One lived in the sea and the other on land. He noticed these iguanas were similar to but also very different from the iguanas he saw on the mainland of South America.

The vegetation of the Galapagos Islands was also very unusual to Darwin. There were tree-size cacti, daisies, and sunflowers. These unusual species baffled Darwin. He could not understand how these plants and animals got to the Galapagos Islands and how similar-looking species maintained slight differences, depending on where they were located.

In 1836 Charles Darwin finally arrived home in England. Once he received all of his specimens from South America, he organized his field notes. He then began to analyze the information he had collected. He also wrote a book titled *Journal of Researches*, which described his voyage.

While studying his findings, the idea of natural selection started to form in his mind. He knew many people would reject the idea because it went against the common beliefs. It took him twenty-three years to finally publish his findings in *On the Origin of Species by Means of Natural Selection*, also known as *The Origin of Species*.

THE SETTLEMENTS OF THE GALAPAGOS ISLANDS

The Galapagos Islands were very difficult to farm because of the rough terrain and lack of water. Few people wanted to settle in this harsh environment. The first islands to be settled were San Cristóbal and Floreana, in the early 1800s. Later, a small village called Villamil was established on southern Isabela.

One of the first islands to be ▶▶
settled was San Cristóbal.

Other villages began to form. Puerto Ayora on Santa Cruz, which is currently the largest town on the islands, was established in the 1920s. In 1926 there were 150 people living on Santa Cruz Island.

Until the 1930s there was no protection for the unusual animals on the Galapagos Islands. Due to their unique qualities, in 1934 the Ecuadorian government passed the first of several laws designed to protect them. This law made it illegal to kill or capture tortoises, fur seals, sea lions, iguanas, and a variety of birds. This law marked the beginning of conservation on the Galapagos Islands.

A land iguana shares the Isla Baltra Airport with a passenger jet.

In 1941 an agreement was made between the United States and Ecuador for the United States to use Baltra Island as a military base. In January 1942 the base was completed. Its purpose was to protect the Panama Canal during World War II. This base was used from 1942 to 1946. When the United States evacuated the area, the airport on base was given to the Ecuadorian government. Baltra Airport is still in use today.

Immigration to the islands began slowly. Norwegians arrived along with mainland Ecuadorians, Americans, and Europeans. In 1937 four brothers of the Angermeyer family arrived on Santa Cruz from Germany. Today, descendants of these brothers work as guides and run hotels, restaurants, and yachts in the tourism industry.

Tourism began very slowly in these unique islands. One of their famous early visitors was President Franklin Delano Roosevelt, who visited the islands on a fishing expedition in 1938.

Up until the 1940s the permanent population on all the islands remained about the same, at six hundred residents. From 1949 to 1970 the population grew to about four thousand people with the first wave of Ecuadorians arriving on the Galapagos Islands. This population growth occurred because Galapagos offered employment opportunities, especially on the farms and in the fishing industry.

Organized tourism did not take off until the 1970s. Before then, it was very difficult and sometimes frightening to get to the islands. One traveler in 1968 tells how he flew aboard a twin-engine patrol plane that dated back to World War II. The seats were made of nothing more than flimsy mesh. There were also several holes in the bottom of the plane. Passengers could look through them and see the ocean below.

The second population explosion occurred in the late 1980s. The wonders of the islands had gained international attention, and tourists began flooding the area. Hotels and cruise ships sprouted up overnight. People were needed to clean rooms, serve food, work as

As tourists flocked to the Galapagos Islands, many Ecuadorians populated them to meet the needs of the growing tourism industry.

tour guides, and perform many other jobs. Ecuadorians migrated to the Galapagos Islands in great numbers to fill these jobs.

The extra people began to put pressure on the scarce resources of the Galapagos Islands. To support these people, more cargo was shipped to the islands, which often brought new species. Both of these factors threatened the Galapagos Islands' **ecosystem**.

OUTSIDE COMMUNICATION

Even though people moved to the Galapagos Islands, communication with the outside world was extremely limited and unreliable.

At one time, locals had to use government phone company booths, which still exist today. These phones had a terrible connection. It was so poor that it was hard to know who was on the other end. One resident remembers, "Prior to the new phone system, it was hard to tell if I was talking to my mother, my wife, or my brother. The connection was that bad."

In 1994 phone service came along with a new local bank in Puerto Ayora, Santa Cruz. The connection was better, but the price of a call was high. It cost $20 to make a three-minute call. Marine iguanas and sometimes sea lions took naps in front of the bank. It was not uncommon for locals to have to push these animals out of the way to get into the bank to make a phone call.

During this time ham radios were the main means of outside communication. A ham radio is a long-distance radio that allows the operator to communicate with other people who own similar equipment around the world. Some local residents became quite skilled and well known for their use of ham radios.

It was not until 1999 that an efficiently working phone was installed. A local resident recalls what happened when the current government phone system was established. "I remember the first overseas phone call where I could clearly hear who was speaking. It was in 1999, when a digitized phone system was installed." And now there is access to e-mail and the Internet. Galapagos is no longer an isolated archipelago in the Pacific Ocean. Today, it is connected to the world.

FIVE

Living on the Enchanted Isles

Five of the islands are inhabited. They are Isabela, Santa Cruz, San Cristóbal, Baltra, and Floreana. Today, there are about 25,000 permanent residents living on the islands. A permanent resident has the legal right to live and work freely on the islands. Everyone else is considered a visitor. This includes Ecuadorians from the mainland.

The capital of the Galapagos Islands is Puerto Baquerizo Moreno, which is located on the island of San Cristóbal. However, the largest town, Puerto Ayora, is located on Santa Cruz Island.

A restricted national park comprises 97 percent of the islands. The only way to visit these areas is on a boat while accompanied by a naturalist who is licensed by the Galapagos National Park Service.

Tourism has become more and more popular. In 2006 more than 120,000 tourists arrived on the islands to experience their natural wonders.

A man rides his horse in the highlands of Santa Cruz Island.

THE LOCAL POPULATION

There are no indigenous people of the Galapagos Islands. Instead, the entire population consists of immigrants from mainland Ecuador and other countries. The majority of people live in or around towns, with a small number living in rural areas.

The population of the Galapagos is increasing rapidly. It is estimated that by 2014, there will be 40,000 people living on the islands.

Some residents of the Galapagos Islands earn their living as tour guides.

Most people work in the tourism industry. Jobs directly generated by tourism include those on cruise ships, in transportation, souvenir shops, in hotels, and as tour guides. Jobs indirectly generated by tourism include those in laundries, bulk food suppliers, Internet cafes, and restaurants. Locals also work in construction, public transportation, and commerce, such as banking. Fishing is another growing industry that is being monitored closely by the Galapagos National Park Service.

Groups of landless agricultural workers also live on the islands. These workers help local farmers grow crops for sale at local markets. These crops include coffee, limes, lemons, guavas, bananas, yucca, tomatoes, lettuce, pineapples, and sugarcane. Livestock and their products are also produced on the Galapagos Islands and include beef, chicken, eggs, milk, cheese, and yogurt.

Together, these immigrants have begun to make a community. They have even created a local newspaper, *El Colono*, that is published monthly. It contains local stories as well as information about upcoming events on the various inhabited islands.

EDUCATION

About 40 percent of the people living on the Galapagos Islands are under eighteen years old. A variety of primary and secondary schools have been established for the children living there. Attendance in these schools is high, but the quality of instruction tends to be low. Students on the islands do learn basic reading and writing skills but generally score poorly in math. Wealthier parents send their children to private schools on the islands or to the mainland to attend secondary school.

Recently, college resources have developed on the Galapagos Islands. Students can attend the branches of the University of San Francisco Quito and Central University located on the islands. Scholarships and discounted tuition are offered to exceptional local students.

Affiliated with the University of San Francisco Quito is the Galapagos Academic Institute for the Arts and Sciences. It was established in January 2002. Its purpose is to educate the Galapagos

Many children living on the Galapagos Islands attend primary and secondary school.

community in environmental management. In addition, it trains island youth in skills that can lead to jobs benefiting conservation of the Galapagos Islands. It also has a program for foreign students who are studying conservation, ecology, marine biology, and evolutionary biology.

The Charles Darwin Foundation is another source of education. It encourages Ecuadorian students to come to the foundation as volunteers. These students work with scientists on various conservation programs. The foundation also has internships for Galapagos students. More than one thousand students have worked at the research station since the 1970s, gaining invaluable career experience.

TRANSPORTATION

The majority of vehicles found in the Galapagos Islands are four-wheel-drive pickup trucks. Many of these trucks on Santa Cruz are taxis. They charge $1 for any ride within Puerto Ayora. An inexpensive way to get around the island is to take a public bus. There is daily bus and boat service from Puerto Ayora to the Baltra Airport. Locals usually use mopeds, motorcycles, or bicycles for transportation.

There are three airports on the Galapagos Islands. They are located in Baltra, San Cristóbal, and Isabela. Two Ecuadorian airlines fly to the islands: TAME and Aerogal. In 1970 TAME was the first airline to begin regular flights to Baltra.

VISITING TOURISTS

Thousands of tourists pour through the airports of the Galapagos Islands each year. Before being allowed to enter the islands, all cargo and luggage, including carry-on bags, are searched for introduced plants or bugs. If anything is discovered, it is placed in **quarantine**.

In order to conserve the natural wonders found on the islands, a list of park rules have been made. Some of these rules are always be accompanied by a licensed guide; do not take any plants, animals, or rocks from the islands; do not touch the animals; do not leave marked paths; do not throw garbage into the ocean; do not write your name on any rocks or walls; and obtain a permit to camp.

The park rules are made not only to protect the park but also to

protect the visitors. Accidents have occurred on the islands that have resulted in injury and death. These accidents have occurred when divers left a group or did not follow instructions, visitors swam in areas marked as dangerous, or tourists did not follow marked paths. Since 1990 seventeen people have disappeared on Santa Cruz Island.

In order to protect the islands, tourists must obey park rules and regulations.

Even though several of these people were found, the rugged terrain, hot sun, and lack of water has claimed lives. To emphasize the dangers, one sign has been posted in the Santa Cruz highlands that states "Stop. Do not go beyond this point. You could die."

LOCAL RESIDENTS AND WILDLIFE

Even though the wildlife in Puerto Ayora is not as numerous as it is on some of the outer islands, unusual Galapagos animals can still be found mingling with humans in this bustling coastal town.

On a windowsill next to a restaurant several marine iguanas lay in the sun, sleeping. In the busy harbor marine iguanas can be seen swimming among the moored boats, looking like graceful sea

Marine iguanas find a free meal in the yard of a local.

serpents. Near the entrance to the main bank in town, a sea lion sleeps on a ledge, while bright orange Sally light-foot crabs scamper up man-made walls.

The fresh fish market is located on the new dock along the main avenue, Charles Darwin Avenue. It consists of two large tables. Local fishermen arrive between 4:00 and 4:30 P.M. with their daily catch of red snapper, tuna, or octopus. The fish are placed on the tables and are swiftly gutted and chopped up. A woman stands by with a tree branch, waving toward the fish to keep the swarms of flies off.

Pelicans and frigate birds eagerly wait for free handouts. Six to seven pelicans might gather around a table. Their back feathers quiver as if in anticipation of upcoming food. When a fish's head, guts, or skin is tossed into the air, huge pelican beaks fight to grab it first. Sometimes a pelican will shove its beak down another pelican's mouth to get the leftover fish parts, while frigate birds quietly glide through the air above the noise, looking for pieces of fish to steal from other birds.

SIX

Saving a World Treasure

One of the greatest challenges in the Galapagos Islands is conserving their natural treasures. Even though the islands belong to Ecuador, their environment and their needs are different from those of the mainland. Because of this, it was necessary to make a law that applies only to the Galapagos Islands.

SPECIAL LAW FOR THE GALAPAGOS ISLANDS

In 1998 a special law was passed by the government of Ecuador that applied only to the Galapagos Islands. This law covers such issues as stopping introduced species from coming to the islands, setting fishing limitations, and implementing conservation programs within local schools. These programs promote and motivate students to participate in the conservation of their home.

One section of the law restricts immigration by Ecuadorians to the Galapagos Islands. Another section expands the marine reserve surrounding the islands. The law also gives a greater percentage of money collected from visiting tourists back to protecting the park.

The natural treasures of the Galapagos Islands are unlike any place on earth.

Groups Protecting the Galapagos Islands

The Galapagos National Park Service was established in 1968 by the Ecuadorian government. The park service's mission is to protect, conserve, and manage the islands' different **ecosystems**. This includes the plants and animals of the islands. In addition, it provides conservation education for all people who visit and live on the islands.

The first two park officials arrived on the Galapagos Islands in 1968. Since then, the park service has expanded. In 2007 there were about 150 rangers.

The Charles Darwin Foundation was established in 1959. The foundation manages the Charles Darwin Research Station, based on Santa Cruz Island. There are more than one hundred scientists, educators, research students, volunteers, and support staff at the station. The foundation's mission is to carry out and oversee scientific research. In turn, this research helps the Ecuadorian government to conserve the fragile ecosystems of the Galapagos Islands. The Galapagos National Park Service and the Charles Darwin Foundation work together. The foundation gives recommendations based on scientific research to the park service in regard to conservation and management. This helps the park service define how to manage the archipelago and reach its conservation goals. The Charles Darwin Research Station staff is also very involved in educating the local community about conservation.

The Galapagos Conservation Trust in the United Kingdom and the Galapagos Conservancy in the United States also help the Galapagos Islands. Both organizations are "Friends of Galapagos" that help to raise money and awareness for the Charles Darwin Foundation and the Galapagos National Park Service.

INTRODUCED ANIMALS

Galapagos giant tortoises are no longer used as food, as they are now protected by law. But animals introduced by humons have continued to affect the giant tortoise population. Some examples are cattle and donkeys that crush tortoise nests, pigs and dogs that raid tortoise nests to eat the eggs, and black rats that attack and eat the hatchlings as they emerge from their shells. One of the most severe cases was on Pinzón Island, where black rats killed all the wild tortoise hatchlings. Introduced fire ants have also been known to kill hatchlings and eggs. Scientists soon realized that if these problems were not solved, there would be no tortoises on the Galapagos Islands in the future.

Programs were established to remove introduced animals that

Tortoise Breeding Program

To save the tortoise population from introduced species, scientists and park wardens gather tortoise eggs from their nesting sites. The eggs are placed in an **incubator** at the Charles Darwin Research Station. Once an egg hatches, the hatchling is put in a dark box for up to four weeks. A colored number is also painted on its carapace. This number identifies from which island the tortoise originated. After a tortoise's carapace reaches about 8 inches (20 cm), it is thought to be "rat proof." The tortoise is then placed in an adaptation pen until it is about three to five years old. At that time it is taken back to its home island. Today, almost four thousand tortoises have been raised in captivity and repatriated to their island homes.

could harm the Galapagos giant tortoise. One such program involved the Galapagos National Park Service hiring hunters. The hunters were instructed to remove approximately 200,000 feral goats living on northern Isabela and Santiago islands. This program was a success. In July 2006 it was announced that there were no more goats living on Santiago and almost none left on northern Isabela. Because of these efforts the Galapagos giant tortoises and their habitats have a greater chance of surviving. Even so, much more work needs to be done to guarantee their future and restore their islands.

Another Galapagos animal that came under attack by introduced species was the land iguana. In 1976 at Conway Bay on Santa Cruz Island, about five hundred land iguanas were killed by feral dogs. This attack almost wiped out an entire colony. There were only around sixty survivors. A short time later, at Cartago Bay on Isabela, another group of land iguanas was attacked. The Charles Darwin Research Station and the Galapagos National Park Service quickly got to work. All surviving land iguanas were rescued, and an iguana captive breeding program was put into place on Santa Cruz. In 1988 repatriation of the land iguanas began. However, it will take decades to undo the damage caused by the feral dog attacks, which only took hours. Anyone can help the animals on the Galapagos Islands by joining "Friends of Galapagos" groups, which operate around the world.

◀ *Through rescue and captive breeding programs, the land iguanas on Santa Cruz Island have a chance of restoring their population.*

Pest Control

The cottony cushion scale insect arrived on San Cristóbal Island in 1982. This insect is originally from Australia, but it arrived on the island via cargo coming from the mainland of Ecuador. Once it arrived on San Cristóbal, it quickly spread to fifteen other islands. It attacked sixty-nine species of plants. Six of these plants were endangered, and sixteen were threatened. But one of the plants worst hit was the native white mangrove. The insect kills plants by sucking out their sap, which in turn causes the leaves of the plants to fall off. This makes branches or entire trees wither and die.

To rid the Galapagos Islands of the cottony cushion scale insect, scientists at the Charles Darwin Research Station were faced with a dilemma. The insect could not be killed by chemicals. One way to get rid of it was by introducing the Australian ladybug, which has been used for pest control in more than sixty countries.

Scientists decided to study what effects the introduced Australian ladybug would have on the Galapagos Islands' environment. Once they had all the information, it was recommended to the Galapagos National Park Service that the Australian ladybug be introduced. These ladybugs were first released in January 2002 on Santa Cruz, San Cristóbal, Isabela, and Floreana. Since then the ladybugs have been released on other infected islands. So far the results have been good. There has been a major reduction in cottony cushion scale insects and the mangrove trees are recovering.

POLLUTION

With humans comes garbage, and unfortunately this also holds true on the Galapagos Islands. Not only does waste arrive from around the world on ocean currents but it is also produced by the local population and the large tourist population.

Today, garbage is becoming more and more common on the beaches of the islands. Plastic bottles, bags, and other storage containers are seen washed up on the shore around populated areas. This pollution sometimes kills local wildlife. Sea turtles eat plastic bags, possibly mistaking them for jellyfish. Young sea lions play with tough plastic rings and get them stuck around their necks. As the sea lions grow, the plastic rings do not expand and end up choking them.

Garbage disposal on the islands is a problem. One solution is to put garbage in local landfills or dumps. Waste materials are buried at the landfill. This method is a common way to dispose of garbage around the world.

Recently, scientists became concerned about the environmental damage caused by burning trash at waste sites. Because of this, they studied the health of local **lichen**. More than four thousand species of lichen live on the islands. These mosslike plants are sensitive to environmental changes and can be used to monitor the effects of pollution. The study revealed that the environment was being affected badly by burning trash. Scientists recommended finding other solutions for disposing of garbage.

Currently, there are several waste management programs being implemented. On Santa Cruz there is a household garbage separation and collection system. It forces residents to separate organic, recyclable, and nonrecyclable garbage. In addition, there are awareness programs in place for local residents.

One such program, held during the summer, is called Happy Vacations, or Vacaciones Felices in Spanish. This weeklong program is for children ages five to thirteen. They are divided into different age groups. Each year a theme is selected, such as introduced animals or the impact of the human population in the Galapagos. Some activities include visiting a recycling center and then creating masks, puppets, and other handicrafts out of recycled materials. The children also have campouts and visit famous sites on the islands,

A sea lion rests near garbage that has washed ashore.

such as the lava tunnels. The final night is an evening of entertainment prepared by the children for the community. During this time there are puppet shows, plays, and games.

There are several educational programs offered by the Charles Darwin Research Station. One is called "Friends of the Tortoises." Local children visit the tortoise breeding center on Isabela Island to help scientists feed and measure the newly hatched tortoises. They also carry out awareness campaigns to encourage people to protect the tortoises.

WATER SUPPLY

Obtaining freshwater was always a problem for early settlers. On some of the islands rain and mist were the only sources of freshwater. This water accumulated in lava basins and eventually evaporated. A few islands, such as Isabela and Santiago, had freshwater springs. But even these sometimes trickled down to almost nothing. Residents had to learn to drink brackish water, a mixture of saltwater and freshwater, from the highlands that traveled through underground tunnels to the sea. This brackish water was free of enough salt to be able to be used by humans.

El Junco Lake, located in the highlands of San Cristóbal, is the only freshwater lake in the Galapagos. It formed from a collapsed volcano cone and is filled with rainwater. Its depth changes throughout the year, depending on the amount of rainfall.

In the 1980s a **desalination** plant was built in Puerto Ayora. This consistent water supply created the ability to provide more people with water. As a result, there was a population explosion and an increase in tourists each year. Some of the hotels also have their own desalination plants, as do many of the cruise ships.

PROTECTING MARINE LIFE

The marine life around the Galapagos Islands is extremely varied and plentiful. The Galapagos Marine Reserve, which extends 40 miles (64 km) off the islands' shorelines, helps protect these animals.

The Sea Cucumber Riots

Sea cucumbers are sluglike creatures that are related to starfish and sea urchins. They live on the ocean floor in the Galapagos Marine Reserve. These sea creatures graze along the bottom of the ocean and feed on small algae particles. This motion helps to **oxygenate** the water for other species and filter debris.

In some Asian countries sea cucumbers are considered a delicacy and are expensive. Fishermen from Ecuador found out about this and in the 1990s came to the Galapagos Islands to fish for sea cucumbers. Some of these fishermen began setting up camps on uninhabited islands. They started to remove the valuable sea cucumbers by the millions from the ocean around the Galapagos.

The Ecuadorian government quickly passed a bill, in 1994, to limit the number of sea cucumbers that could be removed. Fights broke out between park wardens and fishermen. The situation climaxed in violence, in 1997, when a park warden was injured when shot by fishermen at an illegal camp on Isabela Island. The violence continued, with the fishermen slaughtering Galapagos giant tortoises in revenge.

The resolution to the conflict was initiated by the Charles Darwin Foundation and the Galapagos National Park Service. A meeting was set up that brought all parties together to discuss fishing problems and to come up with agreeable solutions. The solutions were put together and added to the Galapagos Special Law in 1998.

This reserve has also been a point of dispute between conservation-ists and local fishermen. Fishermen argued that longline fishing should be allowed. Scientists believed it should be banned within the Galapagos Marine Reserve.

Longline fishing uses a single fishing line that can be up to 20 miles (32 km) long. Attached to this line are hundreds or sometimes

The Galapagos Islands are a natural wonder, watched over by protection groups to ensure the safety and preservation of their nature and wildlife.

thousands of baited hooks. Longline fishing is useful when trying to catch tuna and swordfish in commercial quantities. However, it is known that other sea life, including albatross, sea lions, sharks, stingrays, and sea turtles, can get caught up in the lines, too. Longline fishing has been practiced in the Galapagos Islands for decades. It was first done by local fishermen. This type of fishing then expanded to larger industrial fishing companies. However, in 1998, when the Galapagos Special Law was passed, industrial-scale fishing was banned.

Scientists and other conservationists were extremely concerned about pressure from local fishermen to continue allowing longline fishing in Galapagos Marine Reserve. Therefore, a longline **pilot** program was run by the Charles Darwin Research Station. The results showed that more than half of the sea life caught was not tuna or swordfish. Based on this research, on December 20, 2005, longline fishing was completely banned in the Galapagos Islands.

Local fishermen are beginning to come up with other ways to earn an income. One such way is by developing one-day fishing excursions for tourists. This reduces the amount of fishing and also generates for the fisherman sufficient income to live. In 2007 this program was still in the developmental stages.

FUTURE OF THE GALAPAGOS ISLANDS

After the Galapagos Special Law was passed, the islands began to be managed differently. In the past, plans and programs were introduced from the top levels of management on mainland Ecuador, with little or no local participation by local people and institutions. Today, local residents are encouraged to take part in the islands' management by providing feedback and suggestions and actively participating in conservation efforts. The overall goal is to maintain and restore the plant and animal life on the islands. Money is important in making this a reality, so well-planned tourism is a critical source of income. Local residents, including fishermen, are now considered partners with conservation groups. With all people working together for the protection of the Galapagos Islands, the natural wonders will be maintained. This ensures the treasures found there will remain for many years to come.

Glossary

archipelago a group of many islands

basalt a dark, volcanic rock that forms from melted rock

brackish a mix of saltwater and freshwater

caldera a large, bowl-shape feature created by the collapse or explosion of a volcano's center

carapace the hard upper shell of a tortoise or turtle

concession a right granted by a government

desalination removing salt from seawater

ecosystem all the animals (including humans), plants, and bacteria that create a specific community living in a particular environment

endemic native to a place

feral untamed or wild

flora plants found in a certain place

fauna animals found in a certain place

hotspot a place on the earth's surface where magma rises from deep within the earth, creating volcanoes

Humboldt Current a current that carries cold water northward from Antarctica, up the coast of South America, to Peru, where it then turns westward, toward the Galapagos Islands

igneous resulting from magma or volcanic activity

incubator equipment that monitors temperatures and humidity and provides the best conditions for hatching eggs

indigenous having originated in a certain place

islet a very small island

lichen an organism that looks like dried moss and grows in patches on rocks and trees

magma molten, or melted rock, that is deep inside the earth

naturalist a person who studies plants and animals

natural selection a theory proposed by Charles Darwin in which the stronger and more adaptable members of a species survive and the weaker die out, it is the mechanism that drives evolution

obsidian a dark, glassy rock formed from cooled lava

oxygenate to combine with oxygen

penal colony a settlement made up of prisoners who work as punishment for their crimes

pilot a trial experiment or test performed before something is done on a larger scale

porous full of tiny openings called pores through which fluid can pass

privateers sailors on privately owned ships who are hired to attack enemy ships

quarantine separating plants or animals and placing them in an isolated, sealed place

repatriate to send back to where something originated

symbiotic cooperative; used to describe a relationship between two organisms that is useful to both

tectonic plate one of several large, moving plates that make up the earth's crust

Fast Facts

Official name: Archipiélago de Colón

Other names: Galapagos Islands, Las Islas Encantadas, or the Enchanted Isles

Country: Province of Ecuador

Date of discovery: 1535 by Fray Tomás de Berlanga, the bishop of Panama

Official language: Spanish

Location: 600 miles (970 km) west of Ecuador

Capital: Puerto Baquerizo Moreno, San Cristóbal Island

Largest town: Puerto Ayora, Santa Cruz Island

Total land area: 3,029 square miles (7,844 sq. km)

Highest elevation: Wolf Volcano 5,600 feet (1,700 m)

Lowest elevation: Sea level

Average temperature: 71° F (22° C) during the dry season; 78° F (26° C) during the wet season

Average yearly rainfall: 9 inches (23 cm)

Puerto Ayora

Lava cactus

Population: 25,000 (est. 2007)

Largest island names: Isabela, Santa Cruz, San Cristóbal, Fernandina, Santiago, and Floreana

Famous areas: Fernandina Island, post office barrel on Floreana, Darwin Lake at Tagus Cove

Famous visitors: Charles Darwin, Franklin D. Roosevelt

Unusual plants: Giant prickly pear cactus, lava cactus, poison apple tree

Unusual animals: Galapagos giant tortoise, land iguana, marine iguana, frigate bird, flightless cormorant, Galapagos penguin

Greatest threats: Introduced animals, such as cats, dogs, rats, and goats

Find Out More

....
BOOKS
....
Banting, Erinn. *Galapagos Islands*. New York: Weigl Publishers, 2006.

Jacobs, Francine. *Lonesome George, The Giant Tortoise*. New York: Walker & Company, 2003.

King, David C. *Charles Darwin*. New York: DK Children, 2006.
......
DVD
......
Galapagos. British Broadcasting Corporation, 2007.

....
WEB SITES
....

The Galapagos National Park

www.galapagospark.org

For information about the national park, visiting the Galapagos Islands, park rules, Friends of Galapagos groups, and latest projects.

Galapagos Conservation Trust

www.gct.org

To learn about conservation projects and view fact sheets.

Charles Darwin Foundation

www.darwinfoundation.org

For information about current research projects and the Galapagos Islands' ecosystems.

Galapagos Conservancy

www.galapagos.org

Provides classroom projects and gives information about conservation.

Index

Page numbers in **boldface** are illustrations and charts.

Sara Louise Kras (far left) grew up in Washington State, Texas, and Colorado. She has always loved the outdoors. She enjoys exploring nature and seeing animals in their natural habitats. She currently lives in Glendale, California, with her husband (top right), daughter, and cat. Kras is the author of more than nineteen books for children. She wrote *Antigua and Barbuda* for Benchmark's Cultures of the World series, first edition.

While visiting the Galapagos Islands, she went to the Charles Darwin Research Station and saw the various stages of the tortoise breeding program. She walked along marked paths on Fernandina, where there were great numbers of marine iguana. On South Plaza Island she walked close to land iguanas and watched as they ate flowers from prickly pear cacti. While on Española Island, she saw many blue-footed boobies. Some were doing their mating dance. She watched as they shook their heads up and down while slowly lifting their feet. Off the shores of the islands she swam with whitetip sharks, hawksbill turtles, moray eels, marine iguanas, and sea lions.

"I have always been fascinated with the world. Seeing people, landscapes, and animals different from those where I live is so exciting! Finding out about all the world's treasures and beautiful places and then telling children about them is one of my favorite things to do. I love to get children excited about the world they live in and to get them curious to find out more."